Home Harmony

Harmonize Your Home, Elevate Your Life

By: Jackie Dibble

ISBN 979-8-9901928-2-9

Printed in the USA by Bookbaby

Table of Contents

INTRODUCTION

Meet your home coach, Jackie!

Jackie Dibble is a passionate advocate for home transformation and the founder of the 5D Home Harmony System. With a deep love for everything home-related, Jackie has dedicated her life to helping individuals turn their houses into warm and inviting homes. Inspired by her own journey of overcoming clutter and self-doubt.

Through her love for DIY projects and a desire to share her knowledge with others, she developed the 5D Home Harmony System—a comprehensive guide to creating harmonious and personalized living spaces.

Jackie has a keen understanding of the challenges that come with creating a space that reflects one's true essence. As a devoted partner, stepmom, grandma, auntie and dog lover, Jackie values the importance of family and the comfort of a loving home environment. Her three dogs serve as constant reminders of the joy and unconditional love that can be found within the walls of a well-loved home. Throughout her own struggles with clutter and self-expression, Jackie discovered the power of embracing authenticity and doing what brings joy.

With Jackie's guidance and expertise, individuals can embark on their own journey of home transformation, gaining confidence, clarity, and inspiration along the way. By embracing Jackie's philosophy of authenticity and self-expression, readers can unlock the true potential of their homes and create spaces that nurture their souls and uplift their spirits.

Thank you for allowing me to guide you on this journey!

— Jackie Dibble

INTRODUCTION

Welcome to the Journey of Home Harmony

Your home is more than just a physical space; it's a reflection of your innermost desires, aspirations, and values. It's where you retreat after a long day, where you gather with loved ones to create memories, and where you find solace and comfort in times of need. Your home should be a sanctuary—a place that nurtures your soul and brings you joy and tranquility.

Yet, for many of us, our homes don't always evoke these feelings. Perhaps you're overwhelmed by clutter, struggling with outdated design choices, or simply feeling disconnected from your space. Whatever the case may be, know that you're not alone, and there is a path to reclaiming harmony in your home.

This book is your guide to unlocking the secrets of home harmony through the transformative power of the 5D System: Dream, Decluttering, Design, Do, and Delight. Each step of this journey is designed to help you create a space that not only looks beautiful but also feels truly nourishing and uplifting.

In this introductory chapter, we'll explore the foundational principles of the 5D Home Harmony System and how it can help you transform your living space into a haven of joy and tranquility. We'll delve into the importance of intentionality, mindfulness, and self-expression in creating a harmonious home environment. And most importantly, we'll invite you to embark on this journey with an open heart and a willingness to embrace the possibilities that lie ahead.

Are you ready to transform your living space into a sanctuary of beauty, harmony, and joy? Look no further than the 5Ds of Home Harmony—a comprehensive blueprint designed to guide you through every step of the journey towards creating your dream home.

The 5D System

Let's take a walk through each of the 5 steps:

Dream
It all begins with a dream—a vision of the space you want to create, the atmosphere you want to cultivate, and the feelings you want to evoke within your home. During the Dream phase, you'll tap into your imagination and explore the possibilities for your space, clarifying your desires and setting the foundation for the rest of your home harmony journey.

Decluttering
Once you've clarified your vision, it's time to clear away the clutter and make space for the new possibilities that lie ahead. Decluttering is about more than just tidying up—it's about creating a sense of clarity, calm, and order within your home, allowing you to focus on what truly matters and let go of what no longer serves you.

Design

With your vision clarified and your space decluttered, it's time to bring your design vision to life. Design is where your dreams begin to take shape, as you select furniture, colors, and decor that reflect your personality and style. Whether you prefer sleek modern minimalism or cozy eclectic charm, the Design phase is where you'll infuse your space with beauty, harmony, and intentionality.

Do

Now that your design vision is in place, it's time to roll up your sleeves and take action. The Do phase is where you'll put your plans into motion, tackling projects big and small to transform your space into the home of your dreams. From painting walls and rearranging furniture to DIY projects and renovations, the Do phase is where the magic happens as you bring your vision to life.

Delight

Finally, it's time to sit back, relax, and enjoy the fruits of your labor. The Delight phase is where you'll bask in the joy of your newly transformed home, reveling in the beauty, harmony, and serenity of your space. Whether you're hosting gatherings with friends and family, curling up with a good book, or simply savoring a quiet moment of reflection, the Delight phase is where you'll truly experience the magic of home harmony.

"Your home is more than just a physical space; it's a reflection of your innermost desires, aspirations, and values."

By following the 5Ds of Home Harmony—Dream, Decluttering, Design, Do, and Delight—you'll create a space that not only looks beautiful but also feels deeply nourishing and uplifting. So why wait? Start your home harmony journey today and discover the joy of living in a space that truly feels like home.

CHAPTER I: DREAM

Unlocking the Power of Vision

Your journey to home harmony begins with a dream—a vision of the space you want to create, the atmosphere you want to cultivate, and the feelings you want to evoke within your home. Dreaming is the first step in manifesting your ideal living environment, and it sets the tone for the rest of your journey.

But what does it mean to dream in the context of home harmony? It is not just about envisioning a beautiful house with all the latest trends and gadgets. It's about tapping into your deepest desires and aspirations, and allowing yourself to imagine a space that truly reflects who you are and how you want to live.

Understanding your why—the deeper purpose and motivations behind your desire to embark on the home harmony journey—is key to unlocking its transformative power.

Your vision serves as a guiding light, illuminating the path ahead and infusing your actions with meaning and intention.

At the heart of your why lies a longing for a home that nourishes your soul, a sanctuary where you can find solace, inspiration, and connection. Perhaps you seek refuge from the chaos of the outside world, craving a space where you can retreat and recharge amidst the busyness of daily life.

Or maybe you yearn to create a haven of creativity and self-expression, where your personality and passions can shine through in every corner.

Understanding your why also involves exploring the emotions and aspirations that drive your desire for home harmony.

CHAPTER I: DREAM

What feelings do you hope to cultivate in your space—peace, joy, serenity, belonging? By tapping into these emotions, you can uncover the deeper layers of meaning and significance that your vision holds for you.

Moreover, your why encompasses the impact that home harmony will have on your life and well-being. How will creating a harmonious home enhance your quality of life, relationships, and sense of purpose? By articulating these benefits, you can gain clarity and conviction in pursuing your vision with unwavering commitment and determination.

Ultimately, understanding your why empowers you to align your actions with your values and priorities, guiding you towards a home that truly reflects who you are and what you cherish most. It ignites a spark of inspiration within you, fueling your passion and propelling you forward on the journey towards home harmony. So take a moment to reflect on your why, and let it be the driving force that leads you towards a more fulfilling and enriching life.

CHAPTER I: DREAM

In this chapter, we'll explore the power of dreaming and how it can shape the direction of your home harmony journey. We'll discuss the importance of clarity, intentionality, and authenticity in creating your vision, and we'll offer practical exercises to help you clarify your dreams and bring them to life.

The Power of Vision

Your vision is more than just a mental picture of what you want your home to look like—it's a powerful force that can guide your actions and decisions as you work towards creating your ideal living space. When you have a clear vision of what you want to achieve, you're more likely to stay focused, motivated, and inspired throughout the process.

The power of vision extends far beyond the mere visualization of an ideal home; it serves as a guiding light throughout your entire home harmony journey. With a clear vision in place, you're equipped with a roadmap that not only outlines the destination but also illuminates the path to get there. This clarity fosters unwavering focus, allowing you to channel your energy and resources towards the realization of your dreams.

For instance, if your vision includes a cozy reading nook flooded with natural light, you can use this image as a source of motivation when decluttering your home office, visualizing the end goal as you sift through paperwork and organize shelves. Moreover, your vision acts as a beacon of motivation, fueling your determination and resilience in the face of challenges or setbacks. When doubts arise or obstacles seem insurmountable, you can turn to your vision as a reminder of the transformative potential that lies ahead, inspiring you to persevere in pursuit of your goals.

By constantly revisiting and refining your vision, you can draw upon its inherent inspiration to infuse every step of the 5D process with renewed enthusiasm and purpose.

CHAPTER I: DREAM

Whether decluttering, designing, or delighting in your home's transformation, your vision serves as a constant reminder of the beauty and possibility that lie ahead, driving you forward with unwavering conviction and anticipation.

During the home harmony journey, there may be moments when challenges arise, and the path forward seems unclear. In those times, it's crucial to remember your why and reconnect with your vision—the guiding star that inspired you to embark on this transformative journey in the first place. So, when times are tough, take a moment to pause, reflect, and remember why you started this journey—and let your vision be your guiding light towards a home filled with peace, joy, and fulfillment.

Clarity and Intentionality
One of the keys to successful dreaming is clarity. The more specific and detailed your vision, the easier it will be to manifest it in reality. Take the time to think about every aspect of your home, from the layout and design to the atmosphere and ambiance. What colors do you want to use? What kind of furniture do you envision? How do you want the space to feel when you walk in the door?

Creating your vision for your ideal home is an exciting and deeply personal process that begins with introspection and imagination. To kickstart this journey, start by asking yourself a series of probing questions designed to uncover your deepest desires and aspirations for your living space:

- **How do I want to feel in my home?** Consider the emotions you want to experience when you walk through the door—do you seek a sense of calm and tranquility, or perhaps energy and inspiration? Delve deeper into the emotions you wish to cultivate in your home. For example, if you desire calm and tranquility, consider what specific elements contribute to that feeling, such as soft lighting, soothing colors, or cozy textures. If you seek energy and inspiration, think about how you can incorporate vibrant colors, dynamic patterns, or motivational decor to invigorate your space.

CHAPTER I: DREAM

- **What activities do I envision happening in my home?** Think about how you'll use each space—will you entertain guests in a spacious dining area, or seek solace in a cozy reading corner? Think about the specific activities you enjoy or envision happening in each area of your home. For instance, if you love hosting gatherings with friends and family, imagine creating a welcoming entertainment area with ample seating and versatile lighting. If you value quiet moments of relaxation, envision a cozy reading nook with plush seating and good natural light.

- **What elements of my current living environment do I love and want to preserve?** Identify the aspects of your current home that bring you joy, whether it's the abundant natural light, a favorite piece of furniture, or a cherished artwork. Reflect on the specific features or aspects of your current home that bring you joy and enhance your quality of life. Consider not only physical elements like architectural details or decor pieces but also intangible qualities like the sense of warmth or coziness that certain spaces evoke.

- **What elements do I wish to change or improve upon?** Reflect on the aspects of your current living environment that no longer serve you, whether it's cluttered spaces, outdated decor, or a lack of functionality. Identify the areas or aspects of your current living environment that you find lacking or in need of improvement. This could include practical considerations like storage solutions or layout adjustments, as well as aesthetic concerns like outdated decor or uninspiring color schemes.

- **What colors, textures, and styles resonate with me?** Explore your preferences in terms of aesthetics, considering elements such as color palettes, materials, and architectural styles that speak to your sensibilities. Explore your personal preferences in more detail, considering how different colors, textures, and styles contribute to the overall look and feel of your home. Experiment with mood boards or visual inspiration to help clarify your aesthetic preferences and identify themes or patterns that resonate with you.

CHAPTER I: DREAM

- **How do I envision the flow and layout of my home?** Envision how you'll move through each space, considering factors such as traffic flow, functionality, and spatial relationships. Visualize the spatial arrangement and flow of your home, taking into account how you and your family will move through each space on a daily basis. Consider practical considerations like ease of navigation, as well as design principles like balance, proportion, and focal points.

- **What role does nature play in my vision for my home?** Consider how you can incorporate elements of nature into your living environment, whether it's through indoor plants, natural materials, or views of the outdoors. Explore the ways in which you can integrate elements of nature into your living environment to promote a sense of connection with the outdoors and enhance overall well-being. This could involve incorporating natural materials like wood or stone, maximizing natural light, or creating indoor gardens or green spaces.

By asking yourself these questions and engaging in introspective reflection, you'll gain clarity and insight into your vision for your ideal home. Take the time to write down your thoughts, feelings, and ideas, and use them as a foundation for creating a vision board, sketching floor plans, or compiling inspiration images. Remember, your vision is a deeply personal reflection of who you are and how you want to live—embrace it with enthusiasm and creativity as you embark on your home harmony journey.

Authenticity and Self-Expression
Your home is an extension of yourself, so it's important to infuse your vision with authenticity and self-expression. Don't feel pressured to conform to trends or societal expectations—instead, focus on what resonates with you on a personal level. What makes you feel happy, comfortable, and at peace? What elements reflect your unique personality and style? Trust your instincts and let your intuition guide you as you create your vision.

CHAPTER I: DREAM

Authenticity and Self-Expression
Your home is an extension of yourself, so it's important to infuse your vision with authenticity and self-expression. Don't feel pressured to conform to trends or societal expectations—instead, focus on what resonates with you on a personal level. What makes you feel happy, comfortable, and at peace? What elements reflect your unique personality and style? Trust your instincts and let your intuition guide you as you create your vision.

Authenticity in your home environment fosters a profound sense of joy and harmony by aligning your surroundings with your true essence. When your living space authentically reflects who you are, it becomes a sanctuary that nurtures your well-being and uplifts your spirit. Embracing authenticity invites a deep sense of connection and resonance with your surroundings, allowing you to feel truly at home in your space.

To cultivate authenticity in your home, start by exploring your values, passions, and preferences. Reflect on what brings you joy, comfort, and fulfillment, and incorporate these elements into your vision for your living environment. This might involve surrounding yourself with meaningful objects, artwork, or decor that evoke positive emotions and memories.

Self-expression can manifest in countless ways within your home, offering endless opportunities to showcase your personality and style. Here are some examples of how you can infuse your space with self-expression:

CHAPTER I: DREAM

1. Personal Collections: Display items that hold sentimental value or reflect your interests and hobbies, such as books, artwork, photographs, or souvenirs from travels.

2. Customization: Personalize your space with DIY projects, handmade crafts, or custom furnishings that reflect your unique aesthetic preferences.

3. Color Palette: Choose colors that resonate with you on a deep level and evoke the mood or atmosphere you desire, whether it's calming neutrals, vibrant hues, or soothing pastels.

4. Texture and Material: Experiment with different textures and materials to add depth and character to your space, such as natural wood, cozy textiles, or sleek metals.

5. Artistic Expression: Showcase your creativity through artwork, murals, or installations that express your individuality and spark conversation.

6. Functional Design: Tailor your home's layout and functionality to suit your lifestyle and preferences, prioritizing elements that enhance your daily routines and activities.

CHAPTER I: DREAM

7. Vintage Finds: Incorporate vintage or antique pieces into your decor to add character and charm to your space. Whether it's a retro armchair, a weathered farmhouse table, or a collection of vintage signage, these unique finds add a sense of history and personality to your home.

8. Travel Mementos: Display souvenirs and keepsakes from your travels to infuse your space with memories and stories from your adventures. Whether it's a seashell from a beach vacation, a woven basket from a market in Marrakech, or a handcrafted mask from a cultural festival, these items serve as reminders of your experiences and connections to different cultures and places.

9. Family Heirlooms: Showcase family heirlooms and heirloom-inspired pieces that have been passed down through generations. Whether it's a cherished piece of furniture, a vintage photograph, or a treasured heirloom quilt, these items add a sense of history and lineage to your home, connecting you to your family's legacy.

CHAPTER I: DREAM

10. Personal Artwork: Create and display your own artwork or creative projects to add a personal touch to your space. Whether you're a painter, photographer, sculptor, or crafter, showcasing your own creations adds a sense of pride and accomplishment to your home, while also allowing you to express your unique artistic voice.

11. Statement Furniture: Invest in statement furniture pieces that reflect your personality and style. Whether it's a bold, geometric sofa, a whimsical accent chair, or a sleek, modern dining table, these standout pieces serve as focal points in your home, expressing your individuality and taste.

12. Nature-Inspired Elements: Bring the outdoors in with nature-inspired decor and materials. Whether it's a collection of houseplants, a floral wallpaper, or a reclaimed wood accent wall, these natural elements add warmth, texture, and vitality to your space, while also fostering a connection to the natural world.

By incorporating these examples of authenticity and self-expression into your home, you'll create a space that not only reflects who you are but also celebrates your unique personality, experiences, and passions. Trust your instincts, follow your heart, and let your home become a true reflection of your authentic self.

CHAPTER I: DREAM

Embracing authenticity and self-expression in your home will create a space that not only looks beautiful but also feels deeply meaningful and authentic to who you are. Trust your instincts, follow your heart, and let your home become a true reflection of your unique personality and style.

"Your dream is the foundation upon which your home harmony journey is built."

CHAPTER I: DREAM

PRACTICAL EXERCISES

To help you clarify your vision and bring it to life, we've included a series of practical exercises in this chapter. These exercises are designed to help you tap into your imagination, explore your desires, and articulate your vision in a tangible way. Whether you prefer journaling, visualization, or creating vision boards, there's an exercise here for you.

1. Vision Journaling: Set aside some time in a quiet, comfortable space where you won't be interrupted. Take out a journal or a piece of paper and write down your vision for your ideal home in as much detail as possible. Describe the layout, design elements, colors, textures, and atmosphere you envision. Be specific and allow yourself to dream big. Don't worry about feasibility or practicality at this stage—just let your imagination run wild.

2.Create a Vision Board: Gather magazines, catalogs, images from the internet, and any other visual materials that inspire you. Cut out pictures, words, and phrases that resonate with your vision for your home and arrange them on a board or a piece of poster paper. Focus on images and words that evoke the feelings and emotions you want to experience in your space. Once your vision board is complete, display it somewhere prominent where you can see it every day to keep your vision front and center in your mind.

3.Visualization Meditation: Find a comfortable position and close your eyes. Take a few deep breaths to center yourself and relax your body. Now, imagine yourself walking through your ideal home. Picture every detail—the colors, the furniture, the decor, the lighting. Notice how you feel as you move through each room. Are you filled with a sense of peace and contentment? Do you feel inspired and energized? Allow yourself to fully immerse in the experience and let your imagination paint the picture of your dream home. After a few minutes, slowly bring your awareness back to the present moment and open your eyes. Take a moment to reflect on any insights or emotions that came up during the visualization.

CHAPTER I: DREAM

Conclusion

Your dream is the foundation upon which your home harmony journey is built. By taking the time to clarify your vision and infuse it with clarity, intentionality, and authenticity, you'll set yourself up for success as you move forward in creating the home of your dreams.
In the next chapter, we'll explore the next step in the 5D Home Harmony System: Decluttering. Get ready to let go of what no longer serves you and make space for the new possibilities that lie ahead.

"Dream big, plan smart. Each goal is a new room, each vision a home that reflects your truest self."

CHAPTER 2: DECLUTTERING

Creating Space for Harmony

Decluttering is the essential second step on your journey to home harmony. It's about more than just tidying up—it's about creating space, both physically and mentally, for the life you want to live. By clearing away the physical and emotional clutter that weighs you down, you'll make room for new possibilities and experiences to enter your life.

In this chapter, we'll explore the transformative power of decluttering and how it can help you create a more harmonious home environment. We'll discuss the benefits of decluttering, common obstacles that may arise, and practical strategies for getting started. Plus, we'll provide a timeline to guide you through the decluttering process and three exercises to help you get organized and reclaim control of your space.

The Power of Decluttering
Clutter has a way of creeping into our lives and taking up valuable space, both physically and mentally. It can leave us feeling overwhelmed, stressed, and stuck in a state of chaos. But when we take the time to declutter our homes, we free ourselves from the burden of excess stuff and create a sense of clarity, calm, and order.

Benefits of Decluttering
Decluttering offers a wide range of benefits, from creating a more visually appealing and functional living space to reducing stress and increasing productivity. When you declutter your home, you'll experience:

- More space and freedom to move and breathe: Decluttering creates an open and spacious environment, allowing you to move freely and breathe deeply, fostering a sense of liberation and expansiveness.

CHAPTER 2: DECLUTTERING

- Improved mental clarity and focus: By eliminating visual distractions and reducing mental clutter, decluttering enhances mental clarity and sharpens your focus, empowering you to tackle tasks with renewed concentration and efficiency.

- Reduced feelings of overwhelm and stress: A clutter-free environment promotes a sense of calm and tranquility, alleviating feelings of overwhelm and stress, and providing a sanctuary for relaxation and rejuvenation.

- Increased productivity and efficiency: With a streamlined and organized space, decluttering enhances productivity and efficiency by minimizing distractions and facilitating smooth workflow, enabling you to accomplish tasks more effectively and with less effort.

- Enhanced feelings of satisfaction and well-being: A clutter-free and harmonious environment fosters feelings of satisfaction and well-being by creating a sense of order, balance, and harmony, nurturing a positive and uplifting atmosphere conducive to happiness and contentment.

- Enhanced creativity: A clutter-free environment can stimulate creativity and inspire innovative thinking by providing a clear mental space for ideas to flow freely.

- Better sleep quality: Decluttering your bedroom can create a serene and calming environment conducive to restful sleep, leading to improved sleep quality and overall well-being.

- Strengthened decision-making skills: Regular decluttering exercises can help sharpen your decision-making skills as you evaluate and prioritize items based on their importance and utility.

- Reduced allergens and pollutants: Decluttering and regularly cleaning your home can help minimize dust, allergens, and pollutants, leading to improved indoor air quality and respiratory health.

CHAPTER 2: DECLUTTERING

- Enhanced safety: Removing clutter and organizing your space can reduce the risk of accidents and injuries by eliminating tripping hazards and creating clear pathways throughout your home.

- Strengthened relationships: A clutter-free and organized home can foster a sense of harmony and tranquility, creating a more inviting space for spending quality time with family and friends.

- Financial savings: By decluttering and reassessing your belongings, you may discover items that can be sold, donated, or repurposed, leading to potential financial savings and a more sustainable lifestyle.

CHAPTER 2: DECLUTTERING

Common Obstacles to Decluttering

While the benefits of decluttering are clear, it's not always easy to get started. Procrastination often stems from a combination of factors, including a sense of overwhelm, perfectionism, and fear of making decisions. The task of decluttering can seem daunting, especially if you're faced with a large amount of clutter or uncertain about where to begin. Additionally, the thought of parting with possessions can trigger feelings of discomfort or anxiety, leading to avoidance and delay.

Many people form emotional attachments to their belongings, associating them with memories, identity, or aspirations. Letting go of these possessions can feel like letting go of a piece of oneself, leading to a sense of loss or vulnerability. Furthermore, the fear of making the wrong decision or regretting letting go of an item can create a barrier to decluttering. This attachment can be particularly strong for items that hold sentimental value or are associated with significant life events. However, by recognizing that possessions are not inherently tied to our identity or worth, and that memories can live on even after physical objects are gone, we can begin to shift our perspective and cultivate a healthier relationship with our belongings.

Similarly, perfectionism can hinder progress by setting unrealistic expectations and standards. The desire for a perfectly organized and clutter-free home can lead to feelings of overwhelm and paralysis, as the enormity of the task can seem insurmountable. Additionally, the fear of making mistakes or not doing things perfectly can prevent us from taking action. However, by embracing imperfection and focusing on progress over perfection, we can free ourselves from the constraints of perfectionism and approach decluttering with greater flexibility and resilience.

CHAPTER 2: DECLUTTERING

Decluttering Timeline
To help you stay organized and focused, we've created a decluttering timeline that breaks down the process into manageable steps. Follow this timeline at your own pace, adjusting it as needed to suit your schedule and preferences.

Week 1: Getting Started with Small, Manageable Areas
Day 1: Declutter a Single Drawer Start your decluttering journey by tackling a small, manageable area such as a single drawer. Empty the contents onto a nearby surface and sort items into categories: keep, donate, and discard. As you go through each item, ask yourself if it's something you use regularly, if it brings you joy, and if it serves a purpose in your life. Be ruthless in your decision-making and resist the urge to hold onto items out of guilt or obligation. Once you've sorted through everything, wipe down the drawer and neatly organize the items you've chosen to keep back inside.

Day 2: Clear Out a Shelf Move on to decluttering a shelf in your home, whether it's in a bookcase, kitchen cabinet, or linen closet. Follow the same process of emptying the shelf, sorting items into categories, and making decisions about what to keep, donate, or discard. Consider grouping similar items together to create a sense of order and cohesion on the shelf. Utilize storage containers, baskets, or bins to corral smaller items and maximize space efficiency.

As you organize the shelf, take note of any items that may be duplicates or no longer serve a purpose, and consider whether they can be repurposed or donated to someone in need.

Day 3: Tackle a Closet On day three, set your sights on decluttering a closet in your home. Whether it's a coat closet, bedroom closet, or linen closet, start by removing everything from inside and laying it out in a designated space. Sort items into categories based on their use, condition, and frequency of use. Take this opportunity to evaluate your wardrobe and accessories, keeping only those items that fit well, are in good condition, and align with your personal style.

CHAPTER 2: DECLUTTERING

Consider implementing a system for organizing clothing, such as grouping items by category (e.g. tops, bottoms, dresses) or by color, to make it easier to find what you need when getting dressed each day. Donate any gently used clothing, shoes, or accessories that no longer serve you, and discard items that are damaged or beyond repair.

By breaking the decluttering process into small, manageable tasks and focusing on one area each day, you'll make steady progress towards creating a clutter-free and organized home. Remember to celebrate your achievements along the way and stay motivated by keeping your vision of a harmonious living space at the forefront of your mind.

Week 2: Decluttering Larger Areas
Day 1: Declutter the Kitchen Begin week two by tackling one of the most frequently used areas in your home—the kitchen. Start by clearing off countertops and surfaces to create a clean slate. Then, work your way through the kitchen systematically, focusing on one area at a time, such as cabinets, pantry, or drawers. Sort through items, discarding expired or unused food items, duplicate utensils, and broken appliances. Consider implementing storage solutions such as drawer organizers, shelf risers, or hanging racks to maximize space efficiency. Take this opportunity to declutter and organize your cooking tools, bakeware, and dishware, ensuring that everything has a designated place and is easily accessible when needed.

Day 2: Declutter the Living Room Next, turn your attention to the living room—a space for relaxation and socializing. Begin by removing clutter from surfaces such as coffee tables, side tables, and entertainment centers. Sort through books, magazines, and media items, keeping only those that you truly enjoy and intend to use. Evaluate furniture arrangements and consider whether any pieces can be repurposed or relocated to better suit the flow and function of the room. Incorporate storage solutions such as baskets, bins, or ottomans with hidden compartments to corral loose items and keep the space tidy. Take this opportunity to assess decorative accents and artwork, ensuring that each piece adds value and enhances the overall aesthetic of the room.

CHAPTER 2: DECLUTTERING

Day 3: Declutter the Bedroom On day three, focus on creating a serene and clutter-free environment in your bedroom—a space for rest and rejuvenation. Begin by decluttering surfaces such as nightstands, dressers, and shelves, removing any items that don't belong or are no longer used. Sort through clothing, shoes, and accessories, donating or discarding items that no longer fit or are out of style.

Consider implementing storage solutions such as under-bed storage bins, closet organizers, or garment racks to maximize space and streamline your wardrobe. Take this opportunity to assess bedding and linens, ensuring that each piece is clean, comfortable, and in good condition. By decluttering and organizing your bedroom, you'll create a peaceful retreat where you can unwind and recharge each day.

By dedicating time each day to decluttering larger areas such as rooms or zones, you'll make significant progress towards creating a clutter-free and organized home. Remember to stay focused, stay motivated, and celebrate your achievements along the way. With each area you declutter, you'll move closer to your vision of a harmonious living space that supports your well-being and happiness.

Week 3: Finalizing Decluttering and Celebrating Achievements
Day 1: Address Remaining Clutter Hotspots Begin week three by identifying any remaining clutter hotspots or problem areas in your home. These may be areas that have been overlooked or areas that tend to accumulate clutter quickly. Common clutter hotspots include entryways, closets, home offices, and storage areas such as basements or attics. Take stock of these areas and prioritize decluttering them based on their impact on your daily life and well-being. Use the same sorting and decision-making process as before, sorting items into categories and making decisions about what to keep, donate, or discard. Consider implementing systems or strategies to prevent future clutter buildup in these areas, such as setting up designated drop zones for incoming mail or creating a rotation system for seasonal items.

CHAPTER 2: DECLUTTERING

Day 2: Take Stock of Your Progress Midway through week three, take a moment to reflect on the progress you've made thus far in your decluttering journey. Celebrate your achievements and acknowledge the hard work and dedication you've put into creating a clutter-free and organized home. Take stock of the areas you've decluttered and the positive changes you've noticed in your living environment. Reflect on any challenges you've faced along the way and consider how you've overcome them. Use this opportunity to recommit to your decluttering goals and stay motivated as you continue to work towards a harmonious living space.

Day 3: Donate or Discard Remaining Items On the final day of week three, take action to donate or discard any remaining items that no longer serve you. Gather items that you've set aside for donation and drop them off at a local charity or donation center. Dispose of any items that are damaged, broken, or beyond repair in an environmentally responsible manner. Consider recycling or upcycling items whenever possible to minimize waste and support sustainability efforts. As you part with these items, take a moment to express gratitude for the role they've played in your life and the opportunity to pass them on to someone in need. By letting go of excess belongings, you'll create space for new opportunities and experiences to enter your life, fostering a sense of lightness and freedom.

By addressing any remaining clutter hotspots, taking stock of your progress, and donating or discarding items that no longer serve you, you'll finalize your decluttering efforts and create a clutter-free and organized home that supports your well-being and happiness. Remember to celebrate your achievements and stay committed to maintaining your newfound sense of harmony and balance in your living environment.

CHAPTER 2: DECLUTTERING

Week 4: Finalizing Decluttering and Documenting Your Journey
Day 1: Complete Unfinished Decluttering Tasks Begin week four by reviewing your progress and identifying any remaining decluttering tasks that need to be completed. These may include areas that were overlooked during previous weeks or tasks that require additional attention and organization. Set aside dedicated time to address these tasks, focusing on one area at a time to ensure thorough decluttering and organization. Use the same sorting and decision-making process as before, sorting items into categories and making decisions about what to keep, donate, or discard. As you complete each task, take note of the progress you've made and the positive changes in your living environment

Day 2: Final Sweep of Your Home Midway through week four, conduct a final sweep of your home to ensure that everything is in its place and properly organized. Start by walking through each room and visually inspecting the space for any remaining clutter or disorganization. Pay close attention to commonly overlooked areas such as closets, cabinets, and storage areas. Take this opportunity to tidy up any areas that may have become cluttered since your initial decluttering efforts. Consider implementing systems or strategies to maintain organization in the long term, such as daily cleaning routines, weekly decluttering sessions, or monthly maintenance tasks. By completing a final sweep of your home, you'll ensure that your living space remains clutter-free and organized for the foreseeable future.

Day 3: Document Your Decluttering Journey On the final day of week four, take time to document your decluttering journey and the transformation of your space. Consider taking photos or creating a journal to capture before-and-after images, as well as reflections on your experience. Document key milestones, challenges overcome, and lessons learned throughout the process. Share your decluttering journey with friends, family, or online communities to inspire others and celebrate your achievements. Reflect on the positive impact decluttering has had on your life and well-being, and commit to maintaining your clutter-free and organized home moving forward.

CHAPTER 2: DECLUTTERING

By documenting your journey, you'll not only preserve memories of your decluttering efforts but also inspire others to embark on their own journey towards a harmonious living space.

By completing any unfinished decluttering tasks, conducting a final sweep of your home, and documenting your decluttering journey, you'll finalize your decluttering efforts and create a clutter-free and organized home that supports your well-being and happiness. Remember to celebrate your achievements and stay committed to maintaining your newfound sense of harmony and balance in your living environment.

"The journey of decluttering is not merely about tidying up physical spaces; it's a profound act of self-care and liberation."

CHAPTER 2: DECLUTTERING
PRACTICAL EXERCISES

Here are a few exercises to help you tackle small decluttering projects and make progress towards a clutter-free home. These exercises are designed to be manageable and achievable, allowing you to declutter in bite-sized chunks without feeling overwhelmed. As you work through each project, take note of the progress you've made and the positive changes in your living environment. Celebrate your achievements along the way and stay motivated by keeping your vision of a clutter-free home at the forefront of your mind. With consistency and perseverance, you'll gradually transform your space into a more organized and harmonious environment that supports your well-being and happiness.

1. The 5-Minute Declutter: Set a timer for five minutes and challenge yourself to declutter a small area of your home within that time frame. Focus on removing any visible clutter and putting items back in their designated places. This exercise is a great way to kickstart your decluttering efforts and build momentum.

2. The One-In, One-Out Rule: Adopt the one-in, one-out rule for new items entering your home. For every new item you bring in, whether it's a piece of clothing, a kitchen gadget, or a decorative object, commit to donating or discarding one existing item. This simple rule can help prevent clutter from accumulating in the future and encourage mindful consumption

3. The Decluttering Mindset Shift: Begin by selecting one area of your home that tends to accumulate clutter, such as your kitchen counter, entryway table, or bathroom vanity. Set aside 15-30 minutes to declutter this area mindfully. As you work, pay attention to the thoughts and emotions that arise. Notice any resistance or attachment you may feel towards certain items.

CHAPTER 2: DECLUTTERING
PRACTICAL EXERCISES

Challenge yourself to let go of anything that no longer serves a purpose or brings you joy. Practice gratitude for the items you choose to keep and release any guilt or obligation surrounding items you choose to let go of. Take note of how you feel after decluttering this area—do you feel lighter, more energized, or more at peace? Use this exercise as an opportunity to cultivate a decluttering mindset and shift your perspective on the items in your home.

"Less clutter, more clarity."

CHAPTER 3: DESIGN

Crafting Your Home's Aesthetic Identity

Design is the creative heart of your home harmony journey—it's where you bring your vision to life and infuse your space with personality, style, and intentionality. Design is about more than just choosing colors and furniture—it's about creating a cohesive and meaningful environment that reflects who you are and how you want to live.

In this chapter, we'll explore the art of design and how it can help you transform your living space into a sanctuary of beauty and inspiration. We'll delve into the principles of design, the importance of intentionality, and practical strategies for crafting a space that feels truly harmonious and authentic to you.

The Essence of Design

Design is the bridge between your vision and reality—it's the process of translating your dreams and aspirations into tangible elements that make up your home. From selecting furniture and accessories to arranging layouts and colors, every decision you make in the design process contributes to the overall look and feel of your space.

CHAPTER 3: DESIGN

Design encompasses far more than just aesthetics; it's the embodiment of functionality, comfort, and personal expression within a space. For homeowners, understanding the essence of design is crucial as it enables them to create environments that not only reflect their individuality but also enhance their quality of life. Design has the power to evoke emotions, foster productivity, and promote well-being by harmonizing form and function in a way that resonates with the occupants.

One of the key reasons why design is important for homeowners is its ability to transform their living spaces into havens that cater to their needs and preferences. Through thoughtful design choices, homeowners can optimize the functionality of their homes, maximize space utilization, and create atmospheres that inspire and rejuvenate. Additionally, design allows homeowners to infuse their personalities into their spaces, turning houses into homes that reflect their unique tastes, interests, and lifestyles.

Moreover, the essence of design lies in its accessibility to all homeowners, regardless of their perceived design skills or expertise. While some may feel intimidated by the prospect of designing their homes, it's essential to recognize that design is a learnable skill that anyone can cultivate over time. Homeowners can start by honing their observational skills, studying design principles, and seeking inspiration from various sources such as magazines, websites, and social media platforms.

Furthermore, homeowners can leverage the expertise of design professionals, such as interior designers or decorators, who can provide guidance, expertise, and creative solutions tailored to their specific needs and preferences. Collaborating with design professionals not only ensures that homeowners achieve their desired aesthetic but also helps them navigate complex design challenges and make informed decisions about materials, layouts, and furnishings.

CHAPTER 3: DESIGN

Ultimately, the essence of design empowers homeowners to take control of their living environments, transform their visions into reality, and create spaces that are not only beautiful but also functional, comfortable, and reflective of their unique personalities. By embracing the principles of design and approaching the process with an open mind and a willingness to experiment, homeowners can unlock the full potential of their homes and cultivate environments that enrich their lives in meaningful ways.

Principles of Design

Understanding the principles of design is indeed essential for creating a cohesive and visually pleasing home environment. These principles—including balance, proportion, harmony, rhythm, and emphasis—provide a framework for organizing and arranging elements within your space. By applying these principles thoughtfully, you can create a sense of flow and cohesion that enhances the overall aesthetic appeal of your home.

While these principles may seem daunting at first, they serve as guidelines rather than rigid rules, making them accessible to homeowners of all skill levels. Whether you're a design enthusiast or a novice, learning and applying these principles can significantly elevate the look and feel of your home.

Balance is one of the fundamental principles of design, referring to the distribution of visual weight in a space. Achieving balance involves arranging elements such as furniture, artwork, and accessories in a way that creates a sense of equilibrium. There are two main types of balance: symmetrical balance, where elements are evenly distributed around a central axis, and asymmetrical balance, where visual weight is distributed more informally but still feels visually balanced.

CHAPTER 3: DESIGN

Understanding balance helps create visually pleasing compositions that feel harmonious and well-proportioned.
Resources:
- Book: "The Language of Graphic Design: An Illustrated Handbook for Understanding Fundamental Design Principles" by Richard Poulin
- Online Course: "Understanding Balance in Graphic Design" on LinkedIn Learning
- Article: "The Basics of Design: Balance" on Canva Design School

Proportion relates to the size, scale, and relationship of elements within a space. Maintaining proportion ensures that objects and architectural features are appropriately scaled to one another and to the overall dimensions of the room. For example, oversized furniture in a small room can overwhelm the space, while undersized furniture can make it feel sparse and disjointed. Proportion guides decisions about the size of furniture, the height of ceilings, and the dimensions of architectural features, ensuring a cohesive and visually pleasing environment.
Resources:
- Book: "Designing Design" by Kenya Hara
- Online Course: "Designing with Scale in Architecture" on Coursera
- Article: "Proportion and Scale in Interior Design" on The Spruce

Harmony refers to the coherence and unity of design elements within a space. Creating harmony involves establishing a cohesive visual theme or palette that ties together disparate elements.

CHAPTER 3: DESIGN

This can be achieved through consistent use of color, texture, pattern, and style throughout the space.

Harmony promotes visual coherence and creates a sense of comfort and unity in a space.

Resources:

- Book: "Color Harmony: Layout: More than 800 Color Ways for Layouts That Work" by Terry Marks
- Online Course: "Introduction to Interior Design: Creating Harmony in Your Space" on Udemy
- Article: "Creating Harmony in Interior Design" on The Spruce

Rhythm is the repetition or variation of visual elements to create a sense of movement and continuity. Incorporating rhythm into your home design involves establishing visual patterns or motifs that guide the eye through the space. This can be achieved through the repetition of colors, shapes, or decorative elements.

Rhythm adds dynamism and interest to a space, guiding the eye and creating a sense of movement and vitality.

Resources:

- Book: "Repetition and Rhythm in Graphic Design" by Gabriele Franziska Götz
- Online Course: "Creating Rhythm in Your Design Projects" on Skillshare
- Article: "Using Rhythm in Interior Design" on Freshome

Emphasis, also known as focal point, is the principle of design that draws attention to a particular area or feature within a space. Establishing a focal point helps to create visual interest and hierarchy, guiding the viewer's gaze and anchoring the design scheme. Focal points can be created through architectural features, such as a fireplace or a bay window, or through decorative elements, such as artwork or a statement piece of furniture.

CHAPTER 3: DESIGN

Emphasis adds depth and complexity to a space, creating focal points that engage and captivate the viewer.
Resources:

- Book: "Designing for Emotion" by Aarron Walter
- Online Course: "Creating Visual Hierarchy in Design" on LinkedIn Learning
- Article: "Using Emphasis in Interior Design" on Homedit

While mastering the principles of design may require some practice and experimentation, there are many resources available to help homeowners learn and apply these concepts in their own spaces. Books, online tutorials, and design blogs are excellent sources of inspiration and guidance for those looking to enhance their design skills. Additionally, visiting home decor stores, attending design workshops, and seeking advice from design professionals can provide valuable insights and practical tips for improving your home's aesthetic appeal.

Even if you're not an expert in design, there are simple steps you can take to make your home your own. Start by identifying your personal style preferences and incorporating elements that resonate with you, whether it's a favorite color palette, a collection of artwork, or a cherished family heirloom.

Experiment with rearranging furniture, swapping out throw pillows or accessories, and adding plants or decorative accents to infuse your space with personality and warmth. By approaching design with an open mind and a willingness to experiment, you can create a home that reflects your unique tastes, interests, and lifestyle, regardless of your level of expertise.

CHAPTER 3: DESIGN

Here are more examples and suggestions for identifying personal style preferences and finding inspiration for your home design:

Identifying Personal Style Preferences:
- Look through magazines, websites, and social media platforms such as Pinterest or Instagram for home decor inspiration. Save images of rooms, furniture, colors, and patterns that resonate with you.
- Take note of your favorite colors, textures, and materials. Are you drawn to warm, earthy tones, or do you prefer cool, serene hues? Consider incorporating these colors into your home decor.
- Consider your lifestyle and how you use your space. Are you someone who loves to entertain and host gatherings, or do you prefer quiet evenings at home? Tailor your design choices to accommodate your lifestyle and preferences.
- Reflect on your past experiences and memories. Do you have fond memories of a particular vacation destination or childhood home? Draw inspiration from these experiences to create a space that evokes nostalgia and warmth.

Experimenting with Rearranging Furniture and Accessories:
- Try rearranging furniture to create new layouts and flow in your space. Experiment with different furniture arrangements to maximize functionality and visual appeal.
- Swap out throw pillows, blankets, and rugs to introduce new colors, patterns, and textures into your decor. These small changes can have a big impact on the look and feel of a room.
- Mix and match accessories such as artwork, mirrors, and decorative objects to add personality and visual interest to your space. Don't be afraid to showcase items that hold sentimental value or reflect your hobbies and interests.

CHAPTER 3: DESIGN

Adding Plants and Natural Elements:
- Incorporate plants and greenery into your home decor to bring life and freshness to your space. Choose plants that thrive in your home environment and complement your design aesthetic.
- Introduce natural materials such as wood, stone, and rattan to add warmth and texture to your space. Consider incorporating these materials through furniture, accent pieces, or decorative accessories.

Seeking Inspiration:
- Visit home decor stores, furniture showrooms, and design galleries to gather inspiration and ideas for your home. Take note of different design styles, color palettes, and decor trends that catch your eye.
- Attend home and garden tours, design exhibitions, and workshops in your area to gain insights into various design techniques and trends. Engage with experts and fellow enthusiasts to exchange ideas and inspiration.
- Explore cultural influences and architectural styles from around the world to broaden your design vocabulary and spark creativity. Draw inspiration from diverse cultures, traditions, and design philosophies to create a truly unique and personalized home.

CHAPTER 3: DESIGN

By exploring your personal style preferences, experimenting with design elements, and seeking inspiration from various sources, you can create a home that reflects your personality, interests, and lifestyle. Remember to trust your instincts and have fun with the design process, allowing your creativity to shine through in every aspect of your home decor.

Intentional Design
Intentionality is at the core of effective design—it's about making conscious choices that align with your vision, values, and lifestyle. Intentional design involves thoughtful consideration of every aspect of your home, from the layout and functionality to the materials and finishes. By prioritizing what matters most to you and focusing on quality over quantity, you can create a space that feels authentic, purposeful, and deeply meaningful.

In addition to considering how you use your space, it's essential to prioritize the emotional and psychological aspects of design. Think about the feelings and emotions you want your home to evoke—whether it's a sense of warmth, comfort, tranquility, or inspiration. By infusing your space with elements that resonate with you on a deeper level, such as meaningful artwork, cherished mementos, or sentimental treasures, you can create a home environment that nurtures your soul and uplifts your spirit.

Focusing on quality over quantity is another key principle in creating a meaningful space. Instead of filling your home with an abundance of possessions and decor items, strive to select pieces that are well-crafted, timeless, and aligned with your personal style. Investing in high-quality furnishings, materials, and finishes not only enhances the aesthetic appeal of your space but also ensures longevity and durability.

When choosing furniture, textiles, and accessories for your home, consider factors such as craftsmanship, materials, and sustainability. Opt for pieces that are made from natural, eco-friendly materials and produced by artisans or manufacturers with a commitment to ethical and sustainable practices.

CHAPTER 3: DESIGN

By prioritizing quality craftsmanship and sustainable materials, you can create a space that not only looks beautiful but also reflects your values and respects the planet.

By prioritizing what matters most to you and focusing on quality over quantity, you can create a space that feels authentic, purposeful, and deeply meaningful. Whether it's surrounding yourself with loved ones, cultivating a sense of tranquility and serenity, or expressing your creativity and individuality, your home should be a reflection of who you are and what brings you joy. By approaching the design process with intentionality and mindfulness, you can create a home environment that enriches your life and nourishes your soul for years to come.

Practical Strategies for Designing Your Home

In this section, we'll provide practical strategies and tips for designing your home with intentionality and style. From creating mood boards and color palettes to arranging furniture and accessorizing, we'll cover everything you need to know to bring your vision to life. Whether you're starting from scratch or refreshing an existing space, these strategies will help you create a home that feels uniquely yours.

Starting from Scratch:

Starting from scratch offers a blank canvas, an opportunity to envision and craft a space that perfectly embodies your unique style, preferences, and lifestyle. Whether you're embarking on a new home build or undertaking a major renovation project, the process of creating a home from the ground up is both exhilarating and full of possibilities. With careful planning, thoughtful consideration, and creative exploration, you can bring your vision to life and create a home that truly reflects who you are and how you want to live.

The first two steps, defining your vision and establishing a design concept, are fundamental aspects of creating a home that reflects your personality and preferences. As mentioned earlier, these steps lay the groundwork for your project and provide a clear direction for your design decisions.

CHAPTER 3: DESIGN

By considering how you want the space to look, feel, and function, and drawing inspiration from various sources, you can develop a cohesive design concept that guides your project from conception to completion. Utilizing tools such as mood boards or Pinterest boards can help you visualize your ideas and preferences, allowing you to communicate your vision effectively and collaborate with others involved in the project.

Building upon these initial steps, you can move forward with confidence and clarity, knowing that you're creating a space that truly embodies your unique style and lifestyle.

1. Define Your Vision and Priorities: Begin by clarifying your vision for the space and identifying your priorities. Consider how you want the space to look, feel, and function, and prioritize elements that are most important to you, whether it's ample natural light, open-concept living, or dedicated workspaces.

2. Establish a Design Concept: Develop a cohesive design concept that serves as a guiding framework for your project. Draw inspiration from various sources, such as magazines, websites, and social media platforms, and create mood boards or Pinterest boards to visualize your ideas and preferences.

3. Create a Floor Plan: Take measurements of the space and create a floor plan that outlines the layout and flow of the room. Consider factors such as traffic flow, furniture placement, and spatial relationships to optimize functionality and visual appeal.

4. Select Key Elements: Choose key elements such as flooring, wall finishes, and architectural features that will serve as the foundation for your design. Consider factors such as durability, maintenance, and aesthetic compatibility with your overall design concept.

CHAPTER 3: DESIGN

5. Invest in Quality Furnishings: Invest in high-quality furnishings and accessories that align with your design concept and reflect your personal style. Focus on pieces that are well-crafted, timeless, and versatile, and prioritize comfort, functionality, and durability.

Refreshing an Existing Space:
Refreshing an existing space offers the opportunity to breathe new life into your home without the need for a complete overhaul. Whether you're looking to update a tired room, revitalize outdated decor, or simply inject a fresh perspective into your living environment, the process of refreshing an existing space is both rewarding and transformative. By reassessing your current space and implementing strategic changes, you can enhance its functionality, aesthetic appeal, and overall ambiance. From decluttering and rearranging furniture to updating finishes and accessories, the possibilities for refreshing your space are endless. With a thoughtful approach and a touch of creativity, you can create a home that feels revitalized, inspiring, and uniquely yours.

1. Assess Your Current Space: Start by assessing your current space and identifying areas that need improvement or enhancement. Take note of any design challenges, clutter hotspots, or outdated elements that detract from the overall aesthetic appeal of the room.

2. Declutter and Streamline: Declutter your space and remove any unnecessary items or furnishings that no longer serve a purpose or align with your vision for the room. Streamline your belongings and focus on quality over quantity to create a more cohesive and visually pleasing environment.

3. Rearrange Furniture and Accessories: Experiment with rearranging furniture and accessories to create new layouts and arrangements that optimize space and functionality. Consider factors such as traffic flow, focal points, and sightlines to create a balanced and harmonious composition.

CHAPTER 3: DESIGN

4. Update Finishes and Fixtures: Update outdated finishes and fixtures such as paint, flooring, lighting, and hardware to refresh the look and feel of the space. Choose finishes and materials that are on-trend and complement your design aesthetic, and consider incorporating sustainable and eco-friendly options whenever possible.

Personalize with Accessories: Personalize your space with accessories such as artwork, textiles, and decorative accents that reflect your personality and interests. Incorporate meaningful objects, family heirlooms, and cherished mementos to infuse your space with warmth, character, and individuality.

By following these strategies, whether you're starting from scratch or refreshing an existing space, you can create a home that feels uniquely yours—a reflection of your personality, preferences, and lifestyle. Remember to approach the design process with intentionality and creativity, and don't be afraid to experiment and make adjustments along the way until you achieve the desired result.

"Design is the bridge between your vision and reality."

CHAPTER 3: DESIGN
PRACTICAL EXERCISES

1. Create a Mood Board: Gather images, colors, textures, and materials that inspire you and reflect the aesthetic you want to achieve in your home. Use magazines, catalogs, Pinterest, or other sources to find visuals that resonate with you. Arrange these elements on a board or digital collage to create a visual representation of your design vision. Use your mood board as a reference and inspiration as you make decisions about furniture, colors, and decor for your space.

2 .Room Layout Planning: Select a room in your home that you want to redesign or refresh. Measure the dimensions of the room and sketch out a floor plan on graph paper or using online design tools. Experiment with different furniture arrangements, considering factors such as traffic flow, focal points, and functionality. Use this exercise to visualize how your design ideas will translate into the physical space and make adjustments as needed to optimize the layout for your needs.

3 Design Objectives Reflection: Take some time to reflect on your design objectives and priorities for your home. What feelings and emotions do you want your space to evoke? What functional requirements do you need to accommodate? Make a list of your design objectives and rank them in order of importance. Use this exercise to clarify your design goals and guide your decision-making process as you work on your home harmony journey.

Design is the art of bringing your vision to life and infusing your space with beauty, harmony, and meaning. By embracing the principles of design and approaching the process with intentionality and creativity, you can create a home that nourishes your soul and reflects the essence of who you are.
In the next chapter, we'll explore the third step in the 5D Home Harmony System: Do. Get ready to roll up your sleeves and take action as we bring your design vision to life.

CHAPTER 4: DO

Taking Action to Transform Your Space

The "Do" step of the 5D Home Harmony System is where your vision begins to take shape and manifest into reality. It's the phase where you roll up your sleeves, get hands-on, and start implementing the changes necessary to create your dream home. While dreaming, decluttering, and designing lay the foundation, the "Do" step is where the magic truly happens.

As you get your hands dirty and immerse yourself in the process of implementation, you experience a sense of empowerment and agency, knowing that you are actively bringing your dream home to fruition.

The magic of the "Do" step lies in the tangible progress and visible changes that occur as you work through each task and project. Whether it's painting walls, rearranging furniture, or installing new fixtures, every action you take brings you one step closer to realizing your vision.

With each hammer strike, brush stroke, or screw tightened, you witness the transformation of your space unfold, infusing it with new energy, vitality, and personality.

Moreover, the "Do" step is where you encounter moments of discovery, creativity, and problem-solving. As you navigate challenges and overcome obstacles, you tap into your resourcefulness and ingenuity, finding innovative solutions to achieve your desired outcomes. These moments of triumph and accomplishment fuel your motivation and determination, propelling you forward on your home harmony journey.

Ultimately, the magic of the "Do" step lies not only in the physical changes that occur but also in the profound sense of fulfillment and satisfaction that comes from actively shaping your environment to align with your vision.

CHAPTER 4: DO

It's a journey of self-expression, creativity, and personal growth, where every decision and action reflects your values, preferences, and aspirations. And as you immerse yourself in the process, you realize that the true magic of home harmony lies in the journey itself—the journey of turning dreams into reality, one step at a time.

In this chapter, we'll explore the importance of taking action and provide practical guidance on how to bring your design vision to life. We'll discuss the benefits of proactive engagement, the power of incremental progress, and actionable strategies for tackling projects big and small.

Embracing Proactive Engagement

Proactive engagement is the key to making meaningful progress on your home harmony journey. It's about taking ownership of your space and actively participating in the transformation process. By embracing a proactive mindset, you empower yourself to make positive changes and create the home you've always dreamed of.

It's about taking ownership of your living space and actively pursuing the changes and improvements that will enhance your quality of life. Rather than waiting for the perfect moment or external circumstances to align, adopting a proactive approach empowers you to take control of your environment and make meaningful transformations.

One of the most significant benefits of embracing a proactive mindset is the sense of agency and empowerment it brings. Instead of feeling overwhelmed or powerless in the face of design challenges or home improvement projects, you approach them with confidence and determination. By recognizing that you have the power to shape your surroundings according to your preferences and priorities, you're more likely to take action and pursue your goals with enthusiasm.

Moreover, embracing a proactive mindset enables you to overcome obstacles and navigate setbacks more effectively. Rather than dwelling on setbacks or allowing them to derail your progress, you view them as opportunities for growth and learning.

CHAPTER 4: DO

You're able to adapt and pivot as needed, finding creative solutions and alternative approaches to achieve your desired outcomes.

Embracing a proactive mindset also fosters a sense of accountability and responsibility for your home. You understand that creating a welcoming, harmonious living environment requires ongoing effort and attention, and you're committed to investing the time and energy necessary to maintain and improve your space. Whether it's implementing daily habits to keep your home organized or tackling larger renovation projects, you approach each task with a sense of purpose and dedication.

Furthermore, a proactive mindset encourages a focus on possibilities rather than limitations. Instead of fixating on perceived constraints or limitations, you approach challenges with a solutions-oriented mindset, seeking opportunities for innovation and creativity. You're open to exploring new ideas, experimenting with different design concepts, and pushing the boundaries of what's possible in your home.

Ultimately, by embracing a proactive mindset, you set yourself on a path toward realizing your vision for your home. Whether you're embarking on a major renovation project or making small changes to refresh your space, approaching the process with intentionality, determination, and optimism ensures that you'll create a home that reflects your personality, values, and aspirations. With each proactive step you take, you move closer to creating the home you've always dreamed of—a space that nurtures your soul, inspires your creativity, and provides a sense of sanctuary and belonging.

CHAPTER 4: DO

The Power of Incremental Progress
Rome wasn't built in a day, and neither is your dream home. The journey to home harmony is a marathon, not a sprint, and it's important to celebrate the small victories along the way. By breaking down your goals into manageable tasks and making incremental progress each day, you'll build momentum and stay motivated to continue moving forward.

Breaking down your goals into manageable tasks is a powerful strategy for making progress and staying motivated in your home improvement journey. It involves breaking larger, more daunting projects into smaller, more achievable tasks that can be completed in a reasonable amount of time. This approach not only makes your goals more attainable but also helps you maintain a sense of momentum and accomplishment as you work toward them.

To break down your goals effectively, start by identifying the specific steps or actions required to achieve them. For example, if your goal is to declutter and organize your living room, the tasks involved might include sorting through belongings, purging unnecessary items, and reorganizing storage spaces. Break each of these tasks down further into smaller, more manageable actions, such as tackling one drawer or shelf at a time or setting a timer for short decluttering sessions.

Once you've identified your tasks, prioritize them based on urgency, importance, or logical sequence. Consider creating a checklist or task list to keep track of your progress and hold yourself accountable. Breaking down your goals into smaller tasks not only makes them more achievable but also provides a clear roadmap for action, helping you stay focused and on track.

As you begin to tackle your tasks, focus on making incremental progress each day, even if it's just a small step forward. Celebrate your achievements along the way, no matter how minor they may seem. By acknowledging your progress and recognizing your efforts, you'll boost your confidence and motivation to continue moving forward.

CHAPTER 4: DO

Building momentum involves harnessing the power of small wins to propel you toward your larger goals. Each task you complete builds on the momentum of the previous one, creating a sense of accomplishment and forward progress. As you gain momentum, you'll find that your motivation and productivity increase, making it easier to tackle more challenging tasks and overcome obstacles.

To maintain momentum, establish a regular routine or schedule for working on your goals. Set aside dedicated time each day or week to focus on your tasks, and stick to your schedule as much as possible. Consistency is key to building momentum and making steady progress over time.

Additionally, consider using visual cues or reminders to keep yourself motivated and engaged. Create a vision board or inspiration wall featuring images, quotes, or affirmations that resonate with your goals and aspirations. Surround yourself with positive reminders of why you're pursuing your goals and the benefits you'll enjoy once you achieve them.

By breaking down your goals into manageable tasks and making incremental progress each day, you'll build momentum and stay motivated to continue moving forward in your home improvement journey. With persistence, dedication, and a proactive mindset, you'll transform your vision for your home into a reality, one small step at a time.

Actionable Strategies for Success
In this section, we'll provide actionable strategies and tips for taking action and transforming your space. From prioritizing projects and setting realistic goals to managing time and resources effectively, we'll cover everything you need to know to make your design vision a reality. Whether you're tackling a DIY project or hiring professionals for assistance, these strategies will help you navigate the "Do" step with confidence and clarity.

CHAPTER 4: DO

Managing time and resources effectively is crucial in the "Do" step of bringing your design vision to life. Here are some strategies and tips to help you navigate this step with confidence and clarity.
Start by prioritizing your projects based on their importance, urgency, and feasibility. Focus on tackling one project at a time, starting with the most critical or impactful ones. Set realistic goals for each project, breaking them down into smaller, manageable tasks. Establish deadlines or timelines to keep yourself accountable and track your progress.

Create a project timeline or schedule to allocate time for each task or phase of the project. Consider using project management tools or apps to help you stay organized and on track. Break down tasks into smaller, actionable steps and allocate time for them accordingly. Use techniques like time blocking or the Pomodoro Technique to maximize productivity and focus.

Take inventory of the resources you'll need for each project, including materials, tools, and manpower. Create a budget and allocate resources accordingly, prioritizing essential items and optimizing costs where possible. Research suppliers, vendors, and contractors to ensure you're getting the best value for your resources. Compare prices, read reviews, and ask for recommendations from trusted sources.

Start with smaller, more manageable DIY projects to gain confidence and experience before tackling larger ones. Consider taking DIY classes or workshops to learn new skills and techniques. Invest in quality tools and materials to ensure successful outcomes and minimize frustration. Don't hesitate to seek guidance or advice from experts or online tutorials if you encounter challenges along the way.

When hiring professionals for assistance, do your research and gather multiple quotes or estimates from different providers. Look for contractors or service providers with relevant experience, credentials, and positive reviews. Clearly communicate your expectations, budget, and timeline with the professionals you hire. Ask for references or examples of past work to ensure they're a good fit for your project.

CHAPTER 4: DO

Celebrate your successes and accomplishments along the way, no matter how small they may seem. Positive reinforcement and acknowledging your progress can boost your confidence and motivation. Surround yourself with a supportive network of friends, family, or mentors who can offer encouragement, advice, and guidance when needed.

Consider factors such as functionality, impact, and cost when prioritizing projects. Focus on projects that will have the most significant impact on your daily life or overall design vision. Break down larger projects into smaller, more manageable phases or milestones. Prioritize tasks based on their importance and urgency, adjusting your priorities as needed based on changing circumstances or priorities.

By implementing these strategies and tips, you'll be better equipped to manage your time and resources effectively, whether you're tackling DIY projects or hiring professionals for assistance. With careful planning, thoughtful execution, and a proactive mindset, you can make your design vision a reality and create a home that reflects your personality, style, and values.

Celebrating Progress
As you take action and make progress on your home harmony journey, don't forget to celebrate your achievements along the way. Take time to acknowledge your hard work and dedication, and treat yourself to small rewards as you reach milestones and complete projects. Remember, every step forward brings you closer to the home of your dreams.

Celebrating your achievements along your home harmony journey is not just a nice-to-have; it's an essential aspect of maintaining motivation, sustaining momentum, and fostering a positive mindset throughout the process.

CHAPTER 4: DO

Acknowledging your progress is crucial. By recognizing the milestones you've reached and the goals you've accomplished, you reinforce a sense of accomplishment and satisfaction, motivating you to continue moving forward.

Boosting confidence is another significant benefit. Each time you acknowledge your successes, whether big or small, you reaffirm your capabilities and resilience, building confidence in your ability to overcome challenges and achieve your goals.

Celebrating achievements provides positive reinforcement for your efforts and actions. When you reward yourself for reaching milestones and completing tasks, you associate positive emotions with your home harmony journey, making it more enjoyable and fulfilling.

Recognizing and celebrating achievements helps to maintain motivation and momentum throughout the home improvement process. By breaking the journey into smaller, manageable milestones and celebrating each one, you create a sense of progress and forward momentum, keeping you motivated to continue making strides toward your ultimate goal.

Taking time to acknowledge your hard work and dedication allows you to recharge your energy reserves, preventing burnout and ensuring you have the stamina to sustain your efforts over the long term.

Celebrating achievements contributes to a positive mindset and outlook on your home harmony journey. Instead of focusing solely on the challenges and obstacles you may encounter, celebrating achievements helps you cultivate a mindset of gratitude, resilience, and optimism, enabling you to approach challenges with a more positive attitude.

CHAPTER 4: DO

It's essential to prioritize celebration as an integral part of your home harmony journey. Set aside time to acknowledge your achievements, whether it's completing a decluttering project, achieving a design milestone, or simply making progress toward your goals. Treat yourself to small rewards or indulgences as a way of honoring your hard work and dedication. By embracing the practice of celebrating achievements, you'll not only enhance your motivation and mindset but also create a more enjoyable and fulfilling home harmony experience overall.

The "Do" step of the 5D Home Harmony System is where your vision comes to life through action and implementation. By embracing proactive engagement, celebrating incremental progress, and following actionable strategies for success, you'll transform your space into a sanctuary of beauty, harmony, and inspiration.
In the next chapter, we'll explore the final step of the 5D System: Delight. Get ready to step back, relax, and enjoy the fruits of your labor as you bask in the joy of your newly transformed home.

"Ultimately, the magic of the Do step lies not only in the physical changes that occur but also in the profound sense of fulfillment and satisfaction that comes from actively shaping your environment to align with your vision.

CHAPTER 4: D0
PRACTICAL EXERCISES

In the journey of transforming your home, sometimes it's the small changes that make the biggest impact. These quick wins are like little boosts of motivation, offering instant gratification and a sense of accomplishment. In this section, we'll explore three simple yet effective strategies to elevate your space and enhance your home harmony experience. From DIY projects to mindful design tweaks, these easy wins will leave you feeling inspired and empowered to continue your journey towards a more harmonious home. Let's dive in!

1. **DIY Décor Project:** Choose one area of your home that you'd like to personalize and inject with your unique style. Whether it's creating a gallery wall, upcycling furniture, or crafting decorative accents, embark on a DIY décor project that reflects your personality and tastes. Gather materials, follow step-by-step tutorials or guides, and enjoy the process of bringing your creative vision to life.

2. **Room Refresh Challenge**: Select a room in your home that could benefit from a refresh or makeover. Set aside dedicated time each day or week to tackle specific tasks, such as decluttering, rearranging furniture, painting walls, or adding new décor elements. Break the project down into manageable steps and track your progress as you transform the space. Take before-and-after photos to document your journey and celebrate the results of your hard work.

3. **Create a Relaxation Nook:** Designate a cozy corner or space in your home where you can unwind, relax, and recharge. Whether it's a reading nook, meditation corner, or cozy seating area, personalize the space with comfortable furnishings, soft lighting, and soothing décor. Incorporate elements that bring you joy and comfort, such as plush pillows, scented candles, or inspiring artwork. Use this space as a retreat to escape the stresses of daily life and nurture your well-being.

CHAPTER 5: DELIGHT

Basking in the Joy of Home Harmony

Congratulations! You've reached the final step of the 5D Home Harmony System: Delight. This is where you get to sit back, relax, and revel in the beauty and harmony of your newly transformed home. It's a time to savor the fruits of your labor, bask in the joy of your accomplishments, and appreciate the sanctuary you've created for yourself and your loved ones.

In this chapter, we'll explore the importance of delight and how it contributes to a sense of fulfillment and satisfaction in your home. We'll discuss the benefits of cultivating gratitude, mindfulness, and presence in your daily life, and offer practical tips for infusing your home with joy and positivity.

Cultivating Gratitude
Gratitude is the cornerstone of delight—it's the practice of acknowledging and appreciating the blessings and abundance in your life.

Take a moment to reflect on everything you're grateful for in your home, from the simple pleasures like a cozy corner to curl up with a book, to the meaningful connections you share with family and friends. By cultivating gratitude, you'll cultivate a sense of contentment and fulfillment that radiates throughout your space.

Gratitude is not merely a fleeting feeling of thankfulness; it's a powerful practice that can profoundly impact our well-being and overall sense of fulfillment.

At its core, gratitude is about recognizing and appreciating the blessings, big and small, that enrich our lives.

One of the key reasons why gratitude is important lies in its ability to shift our focus from what's lacking to what's present, fostering a positive mindset and outlook on life.

CHAPTER 5: DELIGHT

By acknowledging the abundance and blessings in our lives, we cultivate a sense of optimism and appreciation for the richness of our experiences.

Moreover, practicing gratitude is associated with numerous benefits for physical and mental health. It can reduce stress, improve sleep quality, boost immune function, and increase overall happiness and life satisfaction. Additionally, expressing gratitude can strengthen relationships and foster deeper connections with others.

To incorporate a gratitude practice into your life, consider various strategies. Gratitude journaling is a popular technique where you set aside time each day to write down three things you're grateful for. These can be simple pleasures, moments of joy, or acts of kindness you've experienced. Reflecting on these blessings helps cultivate a sense of appreciation and perspective.

Another strategy is mindful appreciation, where you practice being present and mindful in your daily activities. Take notice of the beauty and goodness around you, whether it's savoring a delicious meal, enjoying a sunset, or relishing a moment of quiet solitude.

Expressing gratitude to others for their kindness, support, and contributions to your life is also important. Whether through heartfelt thank-you notes, verbal expressions of appreciation, or acts of kindness and generosity, showing gratitude strengthens relationships and fosters a culture of appreciation.

Incorporating gratitude rituals into your daily routine can further reinforce this practice. Whether it's starting each day with a moment of reflection or ending it with a gratitude prayer or meditation, making gratitude a habit cultivates a more positive and appreciative mindset over time.

CHAPTER 5: DELIGHT

By practicing gratitude regularly, you'll cultivate a sense of contentment and fulfillment that radiates throughout your life and home. As you reflect on the blessings and abundance in your life, you'll find that even the simplest pleasures can bring immense joy and delight.

Embracing Mindfulness
Mindfulness is the practice of being present in the moment and fully engaging with your surroundings. Take time each day to savor the sensory experiences of your home—the sights, sounds, smells, and textures that make it uniquely yours. Whether it's enjoying a cup of tea in your favorite chair, taking a leisurely stroll through your garden, or simply breathing in the fresh air from an open window, embrace the beauty and serenity of your space with mindful awareness.

Mindfulness is the practice of being present in the moment and fully engaging with your surroundings. It involves paying deliberate attention to your thoughts, feelings, sensations, and environment without judgment. In the context of your home, mindfulness invites you to savor the sensory experiences that make it uniquely yours.

There are several reasons why mindfulness is important, especially in the context of creating home harmony. First and foremost, mindfulness helps us cultivate a deeper connection with our living spaces. By tuning into the sights, sounds, smells, and textures of our homes, we develop a greater appreciation for their beauty and serenity. This heightened awareness can foster a sense of gratitude and contentment, contributing to overall well-being and happiness.

CHAPTER 5: DELIGHT

By acknowledging the abundance and blessings in our lives, we cultivate a sense of optimism and appreciation for the richness of our experiences.

Moreover, practicing gratitude is associated with numerous benefits for physical and mental health. It can reduce stress, improve sleep quality, boost immune function, and increase overall happiness and life satisfaction. Additionally, expressing gratitude can strengthen relationships and foster deeper connections with others.

To incorporate a gratitude practice into your life, consider various strategies. Gratitude journaling is a popular technique where you set aside time each day to write down three things you're grateful for. These can be simple pleasures, moments of joy, or acts of kindness you've experienced. Reflecting on these blessings helps cultivate a sense of appreciation and perspective.

Another strategy is mindful appreciation, where you practice being present and mindful in your daily activities. Take notice of the beauty and goodness around you, whether it's savoring a delicious meal, enjoying a sunset, or relishing a moment of quiet solitude.

Expressing gratitude to others for their kindness, support, and contributions to your life is also important. Whether through heartfelt thank-you notes, verbal expressions of appreciation, or acts of kindness and generosity, showing gratitude strengthens relationships and fosters a culture of appreciation.

Incorporating gratitude rituals into your daily routine can further reinforce this practice. Whether it's starting each day with a moment of reflection or ending it with a gratitude prayer or meditation, making gratitude a habit cultivates a more positive and appreciative mindset over time.

CHAPTER 5: DELIGHT

By practicing gratitude regularly, you'll cultivate a sense of contentment and fulfillment that radiates throughout your life and home. As you reflect on the blessings and abundance in your life, you'll find that even the simplest pleasures can bring immense joy and delight.

Moreover, mindfulness allows us to create moments of peace and tranquility amidst the hustle and bustle of daily life. By taking time each day to engage with our surroundings in a mindful way, we can experience moments of relaxation and rejuvenation that replenish our energy and reduce stress. Whether it's enjoying a cup of tea in your favorite chair, taking a leisurely stroll through your garden, or simply breathing in the fresh air from an open window, embracing the beauty and serenity of your space with mindful awareness can bring a sense of calm

Incorporating mindfulness into your everyday life doesn't have to be complicated. It can be as simple as setting aside a few minutes each day to engage in a mindful activity, such as meditation, deep breathing, or mindful eating. You can also practice mindfulness while performing routine tasks around the house, such as washing dishes, folding laundry, or tidying up. By approaching these activities with a sense of presence and awareness, you can transform them into opportunities for mindfulness and self-care.

Ultimately, mindfulness is a powerful tool for enhancing home harmony by deepening our connection with our living spaces and fostering a sense of peace and tranquility in our daily lives. By embracing the practice of mindfulness, we can cultivate a greater sense of appreciation for the beauty and serenity of our homes and create spaces that nourish our body, mind, and soul.

Infusing Joy and Positivity
Your home is a reflection of your inner world, so why not infuse it with joy and positivity? Surround yourself with objects and decor that bring a smile to your face and uplift your spirits. Whether it's vibrant artwork, cheerful colors, or sentimental keepsakes, choose items that evoke feelings of happiness, love, and inspiration.

CHAPTER 5: DELIGHT

Create spaces that invite laughter, connection, and celebration, and watch as the energy of joy permeates every corner of your home.

Your home serves as more than just a physical shelter; it's a reflection of your inner world, your emotions, and your experiences. Infusing it with joy and positivity can have a profound impact on your overall well-being and happiness. When you surround yourself with objects and decor that bring a smile to your face and uplift your spirits, you create an environment that nurtures and supports you on a deeper level.

Choosing items for your home that evoke feelings of happiness, love, and inspiration can be a powerful way to enhance your daily life. Vibrant artwork, cheerful colors, and sentimental keepsakes can serve as reminders of cherished memories, beloved experiences, and the people and places you hold dear. These elements not only add visual interest to your space but also imbue it with personal meaning and significance.

Creating spaces within your home that invite laughter, connection, and celebration can further amplify the energy of joy. Whether it's a cozy living room where friends and family gather for game nights and movie marathons, a sunny kitchen where you whip up delicious meals and share stories over dinner, or a serene bedroom retreat where you unwind and recharge, each area of your home can be designed to cultivate moments of joy and connection.

Incorporating elements of joy and positivity into your home decor doesn't have to be complicated or expensive. It can be as simple as displaying photographs of loved ones, arranging fresh flowers in a vase, or adding playful accents like colorful throw pillows or quirky wall art. By intentionally curating your surroundings to reflect your unique personality and preferences, you create a space that feels truly uplifting and inspiring.

CHAPTER 5: DELIGHT

The energy of joy has a ripple effect, permeating every corner of your home and influencing your mood and outlook on life. When you surround yourself with positivity and embrace the beauty of joyful living, you create a sanctuary that nurtures your soul and uplifts your spirit. So why not infuse your home with joy and let its radiant energy fill your heart with happiness and contentment?

Celebrating Your Achievements

As you bask in the delight of your newly transformed home, take time to celebrate your achievements and acknowledge how far you've come on your home harmony journey. Invite friends and family over for a housewarming party, host a dinner or movie night in your newly designed space, or simply take a moment to toast yourself with a glass of wine and revel in the beauty of your surroundings. You've worked hard to create a home that brings you joy and fulfillment—now it's time to enjoy it to the fullest.

As you revel in the delight of your newly transformed home, it's important to celebrate your achievements and share your joy with others. Hosting a housewarming party is a wonderful way to gather friends and family to celebrate your home harmony journey. Consider inviting loved ones over for a casual gathering filled with laughter, good food, and shared memories. Use the opportunity to give guided tours of your newly designed space, highlighting the unique features and personal touches that make it special to you.

Alternatively, you can host a themed dinner or movie night in your home to showcase its newfound beauty and functionality. Create a cozy ambiance with soft lighting, comfortable seating, and delectable refreshments. Choose a movie or theme that reflects your interests and style, and enjoy an evening of relaxation and camaraderie with your guests.

CHAPTER 5: DELIGHT

If hosting a gathering isn't feasible, take a moment to celebrate your achievements privately. Treat yourself to a special meal or dessert, indulge in a luxurious bubble bath, or simply sit back with a glass of wine and soak in the beauty of your surroundings. Reflect on the journey you've taken to create your dream home and savor the sense of accomplishment and fulfillment that comes with it.

Sharing your delight with others can also be done virtually through social media or video calls. Post photos or videos of your newly transformed home on platforms like Instagram or Facebook, and share your experiences and insights with friends and followers. You may inspire others to embark on their own home harmony journey or spark conversations about design and decor.

Ultimately, the key is to find ways to express gratitude for your home and share the joy of your achievements with those around you. Whether through hosting gatherings, enjoying quiet moments of reflection, or sharing your experiences online, celebrating your home harmony journey is a meaningful way to honor the effort and dedication you've invested in creating a space that brings you joy and fulfillment.

Sharing your delight and celebrating your achievements with others is not only a joyful experience but also beneficial for your overall well-being. Inviting friends and family to celebrate with you strengthens your relationships and fosters a sense of connection and belonging. By expressing gratitude for your home and the journey you've taken to create it, you magnify the sense of appreciation you feel for your space and the efforts you've invested in making it a reflection of your vision and values.

Moreover, celebrating your achievements publicly or privately allows you to acknowledge your hard work, creativity, and resourcefulness, boosting your self-esteem and self-confidence.

CHAPTER 5: DELIGHT

Recognizing your accomplishments promotes relaxation, enjoyment, and a sense of fulfillment, releasing feel-good neurotransmitters like dopamine and serotonin that elevate mood and reduce stress.

Sharing your delight with others also inspires and motivates them to pursue their own dreams and aspirations. Your enthusiasm and passion for creating a harmonious home can encourage friends, family, and even strangers to embark on their own journeys of self-expression and personal fulfillment.

In essence, celebrating your achievements and sharing your delight not only enriches your relationships and deepens your appreciation for your home but also contributes to your overall happiness and well-being. It's a powerful reminder of the value of gratitude, connection, and self-expression in creating a life that brings you joy and fulfillment.

The Delight step of the 5D Home Harmony System is where you reap the rewards of your efforts and revel in the joy of your newly transformed home. By cultivating gratitude, embracing mindfulness, and infusing your space with joy and positivity, you'll create a sanctuary that nourishes your soul and uplifts your spirit for years to come.

As you continue on your home harmony journey, remember to stay present, stay grateful, and stay open to the endless possibilities that await you in your beautifully designed and delightfully harmonious home.

CHATPER 6: FINAL THOUGHTS

Embracing Home Harmony

As we conclude our journey through the 5D system of creating home harmony—Dream, Decluttering, Design, Do, and Delight—it's essential to reflect on the transformative power of this process. Each step has been a building block, guiding us toward the realization of our vision for a harmonious and fulfilling home.

In the Dream phase, we dared to envision the possibilities, allowing our imagination to roam freely and envision the home of our dreams. Through introspection and visualization, we clarified our desires and set the foundation for our journey.

Decluttering challenged us to let go of the physical and emotional clutter that weighed us down, clearing space for new beginnings and fresh perspectives. We confronted obstacles and embraced the liberation that comes from releasing what no longer serves us.

In the Design phase, we became architects of our own destiny, translating our dreams into tangible plans and actionable steps. Drawing upon principles of balance, harmony, and self-expression, we curated spaces that reflect our unique personalities and aspirations.

The Do phase propelled us into action, empowering us to turn our plans into reality through dedication, perseverance, and resourcefulness. With each task completed, we moved closer to the fulfillment of our vision, overcoming challenges with resilience and determination.

Finally, in the Delight phase, we reveled in the joy and satisfaction of our accomplishments, celebrating the transformation of our homes into havens of happiness and inspiration. We shared our delight with others, spreading positivity and gratitude for the abundance in our lives.

CHATPER 6: FINAL THOUGHTS

As we bid farewell to this journey, let us carry forward the lessons learned, and the memories cherished. Let us continue to cultivate gratitude for the beauty and blessings that surround us, finding joy in the simple moments and profound connections that enrich our lives.

May our homes always be a reflection of our innermost selves—spaces of comfort, creativity, and connection. And may our hearts be filled with gratitude for the journey that has brought us to this place of home harmony.

With deepest appreciation and warmest wishes,